Illuminated Christmas

A Christian Coloring Book

Illustrations by Carolyn Williams

CONCORDIA PUBLISHING HOUSE • SAINT LOUIS

Copyright © 2024 by Concordia Publishing House
3558 S. Jefferson Ave., St. Louis, MO 63118–3968
1-800-325-3040 • cph.org

Manufactured in the United States of America

1 2 3 4 5 6 7 8 9 10 33 32 31 30 29 28 27 26 25 24

This book illuminated by

In the beginning was the Word,
and the Word was with God,
and the Word was God. . . .
And the Word became flesh and dwelt among us,
and we have seen His glory,
glory as of the only Son from the Father,
full of grace and truth.

(John 1:1, 14)

Glory

Prepare the Royal Highway

Prepare the royal highway;
The King of kings is near!
Let ev'ry hill and valley
A level road appear!
Then greet the King of Glory
Foretold in sacred story: *REFRAIN*

REFRAIN:
Hosanna to the Lord,
For He fulfills God's Word!

God's people, see Him coming:
Your own eternal king!
Palm branches strew before Him!
Spread garments! Shout and sing!
God's promise will not fail you!
No more shall doubt assail you! *REFRAIN*

Then fling the gates wide open
To greet your promised king!
Your king, yet ev'ry nation
Its tribute too should bring.
All lands, bow down before Him!
All nations, now adore Him! *REFRAIN*

His is no earthly kingdom;
It comes from heav'n above.
His rule is peace and freedom
And justice, truth, and love.
So let your praise be sounding
For kindness so abounding: *REFRAIN*

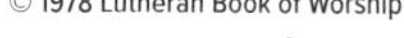

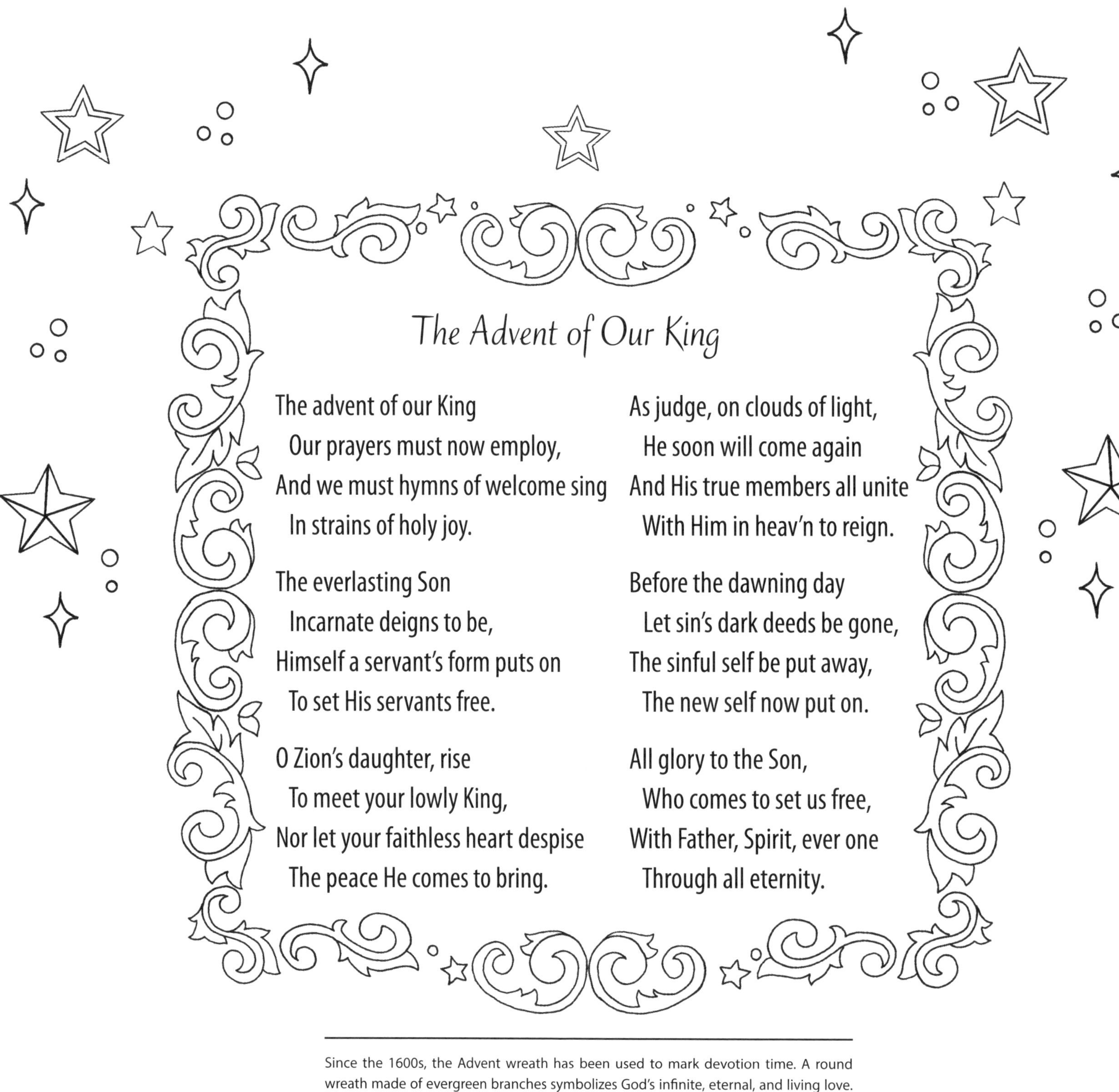

The Advent of Our King

The advent of our King
  Our prayers must now employ,
And we must hymns of welcome sing
  In strains of holy joy.

The everlasting Son
  Incarnate deigns to be,
Himself a servant's form puts on
  To set His servants free.

O Zion's daughter, rise
  To meet your lowly King,
Nor let your faithless heart despise
  The peace He comes to bring.

As judge, on clouds of light,
  He soon will come again
And His true members all unite
  With Him in heav'n to reign.

Before the dawning day
  Let sin's dark deeds be gone,
The sinful self be put away,
  The new self now put on.

All glory to the Son,
  Who comes to set us free,
With Father, Spirit, ever one
  Through all eternity.

Since the 1600s, the Advent wreath has been used to mark devotion time. A round wreath made of evergreen branches symbolizes God's infinite, eternal, and living love. The four candles symbolize the hope, peace, joy, and love that are ours because of Christ Jesus. Three of the candles are blue, the color of Advent, reflecting the hope of the coming Messiah and the second coming of Christ. The color of the third week of Advent, Gaudete Sunday, is rose, indicating our joy that the Messiah has come.

All this took place to fulfill what the Lord had spoken by the prophet:
"Behold, the virgin shall conceive and bear a son,
and they shall call His name Immanuel"
(which means, God with us).

(Matthew 1:22–23)

Immanuel,
GOD
with us,
JESUS,
Behold

O Come, O Come, Emmanuel

O come, O come, Emmanuel,
And ransom captive Israel,
That mourns in lonely exile here
Until the Son of God appear. ***REFRAIN***

REFRAIN:
Rejoice!
Rejoice! Emmanuel
Shall come to thee, O Israel!

O come, Thou Wisdom from on high,
Who ord'rest all things mightily;
To us the path of knowledge show,
And teach us in her ways to go. ***REFRAIN***

O come, O come, Thou Lord of might,
Who to Thy tribes on Sinai's height
In ancient times didst give the Law
In cloud and majesty and awe. ***REFRAIN***

O come, Thou Branch of Jesse's tree,
Free them from Satan's tyranny
That trust Thy mighty pow'r to save,
And give them vict'ry o'er the grave. ***REFRAIN***

O come, Thou Key of David, come,
And open wide our heav'nly home;
Make safe the way that leads on high,
And close the path to misery. ***REFRAIN***

O come, Thou Dayspring from on high,
And cheer us by Thy drawing nigh;
Disperse the gloomy clouds of night,
And death's dark shadows put to flight. ***REFRAIN***

O come, Desire of nations, bind
In one the hearts of all mankind;
Bid Thou our sad divisions cease,
And be Thyself our King of Peace. ***REFRAIN***

With origins dating to the eighth century, this hymn paraphrases the *O Antiphons,* titles and names of the Messiah drawn from the book of Isaiah. Our meditation is aided by symbols and shapes that remind us that God's promise to the children of Israel has been fulfilled in Jesus. The key image is our reminder that Jesus opened heaven to us.

Rejoice!

Come, Thou Long-Expected Jesus

Come, Thou long-expected Jesus,
  Born to set Thy people free;
From our fears and sins release us;
  Let us find our rest in Thee.
Israel's strength and consolation,
  Hope of all the earth Thou art,
Dear desire of ev'ry nation,
  Joy of ev'ry longing heart.

Born Thy people to deliver;
  Born a child and yet a king!
Born to reign in us forever,
  Now Thy gracious kingdom bring.
By Thine own eternal Spirit
  Rule in all our hearts alone;
By Thine all-sufficient merit
  Raise us to Thy glorious throne.

Even as we rejoice that our "long-expected Jesus" has come, we long for His return to "raise us to Thy glorious throne." The crown symbol reminds us that Jesus is indeed the King of kings and Lord of lords. The laurel at the center of the illustration reminds us of the peace that is ours in Jesus. The many hearts remind us that the Spirit, sent by Jesus, "rule[s] in all our hearts." And the Chi-Rho at the center has been used by Christians since the 300s; these symbols are the first two letters in the Greek word for Christ.

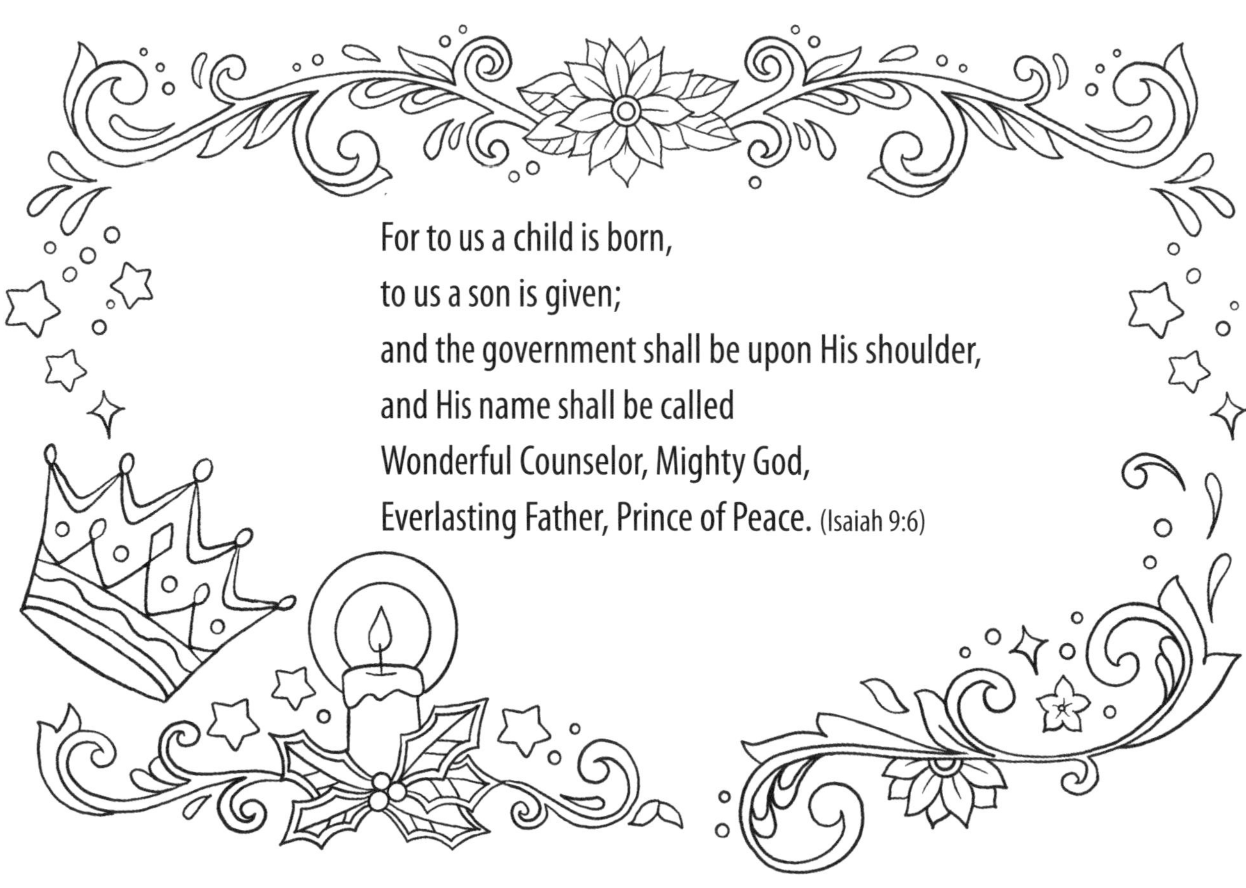
For to us a child is born,
to us a son is given;
and the government shall be upon His shoulder,
and His name shall be called
Wonderful Counselor, Mighty God,
Everlasting Father, Prince of Peace. (Isaiah 9:6)

Wonderful Counselor,
Mighty GOD,
Everlasting
Father,
Prince of Peace

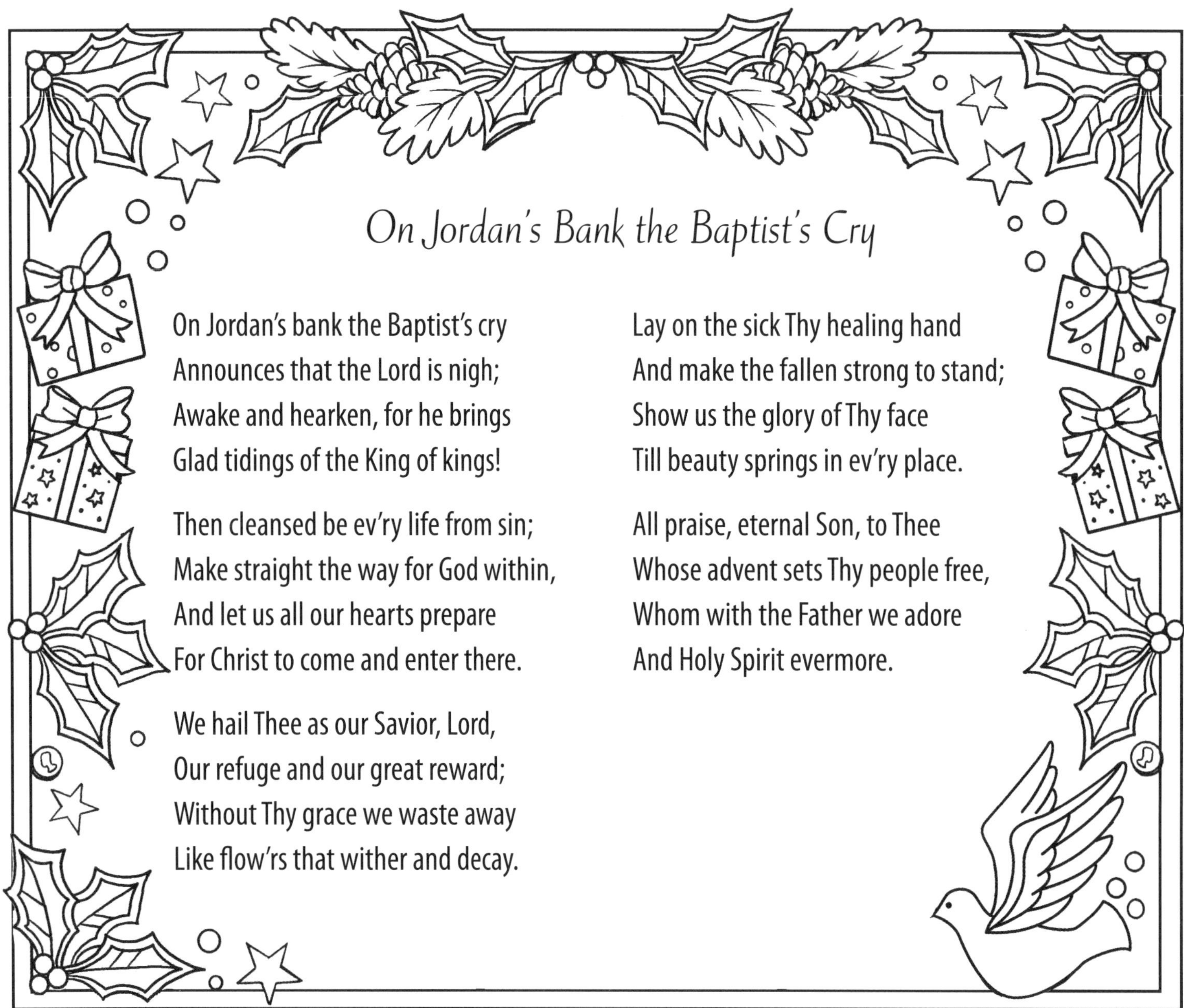

John the Baptist points us to the Lord and helps us prepare for His arrival. Floral shapes remind us of new life in Christ and continual spiritual growth worked in us by the Holy Spirit. Eternity with Jesus is symbolized by circles. Doves are symbols of purity, peace, and the Holy Spirit. At the center of the design is Baptism, which was at the heart of John's message and is a means by which we receive forgiveness and grace. The three drops of water from the shell represent the three persons of the Trinity. This shape is repeated to remind us of our own Baptism.

Savior of the Nations, Come

Savior of the nations, come,
Virgin's Son, make here Your home!
Marvel now, O heav'n and earth,
That the Lord chose such a birth.

Not by human flesh and blood,
By the Spirit of our God,
Was the Word of God made flesh—
Woman's offspring, pure and fresh.

Here a maid was found with child,
Yet remained a virgin mild.
In her womb this truth was shown:
God was there upon His throne.

Then stepped forth the Lord of all
From His pure and kingly hall;
God of God, yet fully man,
His heroic course began.

God the Father was His source,
Back to God He ran His course.
Into hell His road went down,
Back then to His throne and crown.

For You are the Father's Son
Who in flesh the vict'ry won.
By Your mighty pow'r make whole
All our ills of flesh and soul.

From the manger newborn light
Shines in glory through the night.
Darkness there no more resides;
In this light faith now abides.

Glory to the Father sing,
Glory to the Son, our king,
Glory to the Spirit be
Now and through eternity.

A globe has been used since ancient times to represent God's creation in all its majesty and His sovereignty over His creation. Here the symbol stands for the new earth—the new creation—where we will spend eternity with Jesus. The floral motif represents continuous spiritual growth and new life in Christ. The beams, or petals, radiating from the earth remind us of the glory of the Lord, for indeed, Jesus came for all people of all nations.

Hark the Glad Sound
Hark the glad sound! The Savior comes,
The Savior promised long;
Let ev'ry heart prepare a throne
And ev'ry voice a song.
He comes the pris'ners to release,
In Satan's bondage held.
The gates of brass before Him burst,
The iron fetters yield.
He comes the broken heart to bind,
The bleeding soul to cure,
And with the treasures of His grace
To enrich the humble poor.
Our glad hosannas, Prince of Peace,
Thy welcome shall proclaim,
And heav'n's eternal arches ring
With Thy belovèd name.

Hosanna

And the angel said to her, "Do not be afraid, Mary, for you have found favor with God. And behold, you will conceive in your womb and bear a son and you shall call His name Jesus."

(Luke 1:30–31)

The mother of our Lord is a familiar image, especially in Christmas art. Historical symbols associated with Mary indicate her faith, piety, purity, and obedience. The lily symbolizes her purity. The rose, from which we get the word *rosary*, symbolizes her humility and prayer. The gentle blue color, periwinkle, is associated with heaven, peace, and grace. The columbine is a symbol of the Holy Spirit, who overshadowed Mary.

The Angel Gabriel from Heaven Came

The angel Gabriel from heaven came,
With wings as drifted snow, with eyes as flame:
"All hail to thee, O lowly maiden Mary,
Most highly favored lady." *GLORIA!*

"For know a blessèd mother thou shalt be,
All generations laud and honor thee;
Thy son shall be Emmanuel, by seers foretold,
Most highly favored lady." *GLORIA!*

Then gentle Mary meekly bowed her head;
"To me be as it pleaseth God," she said.
"My soul shall laud and magnify God's holy name."
Most highly favored lady, *GLORIA!*

Of her, Emmanuel, the Christ, was born
In Bethlehem all on a Christmas morn,
And Christian folk throughout the world will ever
say:
"Most highly favored lady." *GLORIA!*

GLORIA

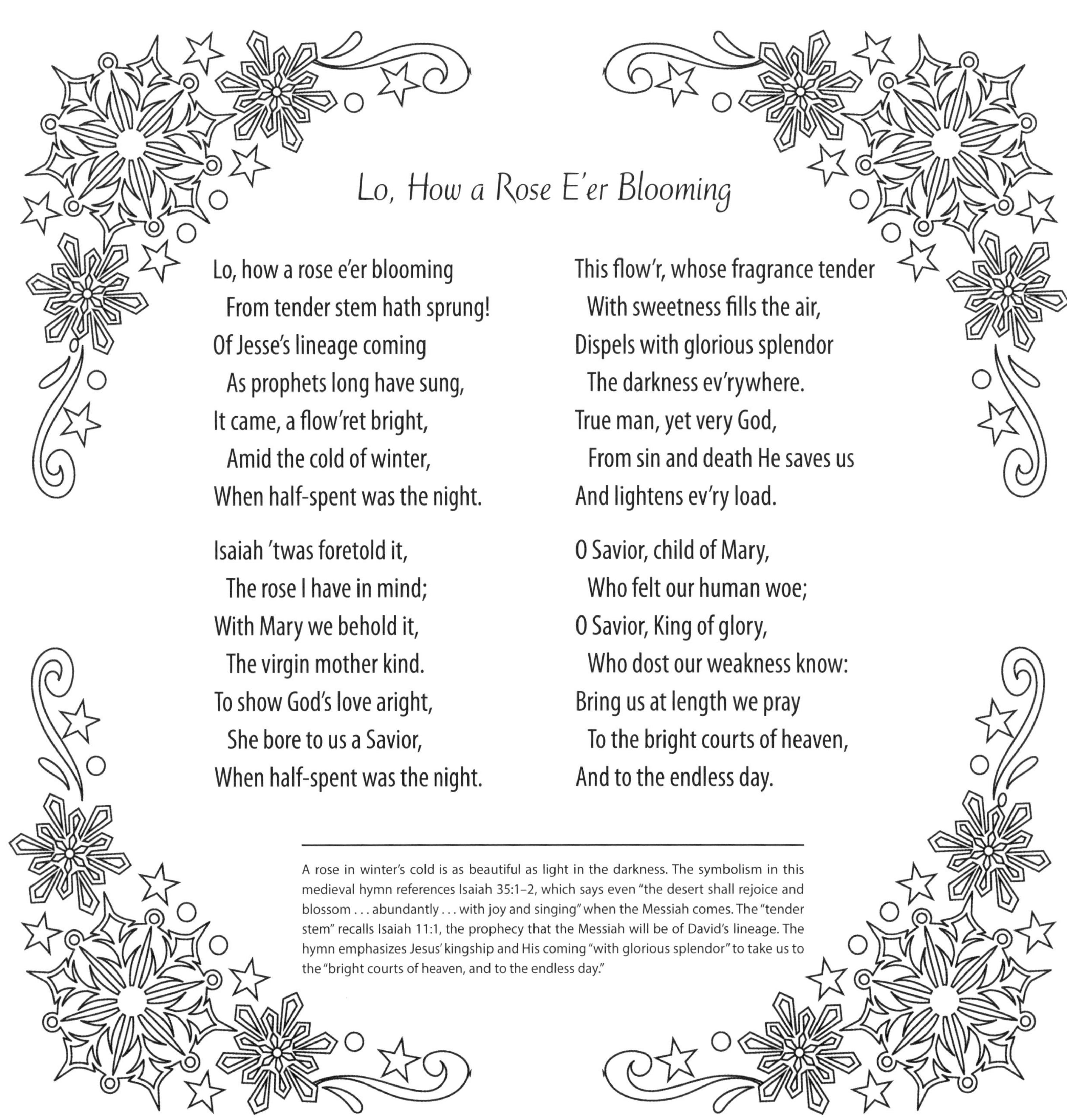

Lo, How a Rose E'er Blooming

Lo, how a rose e'er blooming
From tender stem hath sprung!
Of Jesse's lineage coming
As prophets long have sung,
It came, a flow'ret bright,
Amid the cold of winter,
When half-spent was the night.

Isaiah 'twas foretold it,
The rose I have in mind;
With Mary we behold it,
The virgin mother kind.
To show God's love aright,
She bore to us a Savior,
When half-spent was the night.

This flow'r, whose fragrance tender
With sweetness fills the air,
Dispels with glorious splendor
The darkness ev'rywhere.
True man, yet very God,
From sin and death He saves us
And lightens ev'ry load.

O Savior, child of Mary,
Who felt our human woe;
O Savior, King of glory,
Who dost our weakness know:
Bring us at length we pray
To the bright courts of heaven,
And to the endless day.

A rose in winter's cold is as beautiful as light in the darkness. The symbolism in this medieval hymn references Isaiah 35:1–2, which says even "the desert shall rejoice and blossom . . . abundantly . . . with joy and singing" when the Messiah comes. The "tender stem" recalls Isaiah 11:1, the prophecy that the Messiah will be of David's lineage. The hymn emphasizes Jesus' kingship and His coming "with glorious splendor" to take us to the "bright courts of heaven, and to the endless day."

And she gave birth to her firstborn son and wrapped
Him in swaddling cloths and laid Him in a manger,
because there was no place for them in the inn.
(Luke 2:7)

Gentle Mary Laid Her Child

Gentle Mary laid her child
  Lowly in a manger;
There He lay, the Undefiled,
  To the world a stranger.
Such a babe in such a place,
  Can He be the Savior?
Ask the saved of all the race
  Who have found His favor.

Angels sang about His birth,
  Wise Men sought and found Him;
Heaven's star shone brightly forth
  Glory all around Him.
Shepherds saw the wondrous sight,
  Heard the angels singing;
All the plains were lit that night,
  All the hills were ringing.

Gentle Mary laid her child
  Lowly in a manger;
He is still the Undefiled
  But no more a stranger.
Son of God of humble birth,
  Beautiful the story;
Praise His name in all the earth;
  Hail the King of glory!

Away in a Manger

Away in a manger, no crib for a bed,
The little Lord Jesus laid down His sweet head.
The stars in the [bright] sky looked down where He lay,
The little Lord Jesus asleep on the hay.

The cattle are lowing, the baby awakes,
But little Lord Jesus, no crying He makes.
I love Thee, Lord Jesus! Look down from the sky,
And stay by my cradle till morning is nigh.

Be near me, Lord Jesus; I ask Thee to stay
Close by me forever and love me, I pray.
Bless all the dear children in Thy tender care,
And take us to heaven to live with Thee there.

Silent Night, Holy Night

Silent night, holy night!
All is calm, all is bright
Round yon virgin mother and child.
Holy Infant, so tender and mild,
  Sleep in heavenly peace,
  Sleep in heavenly peace.

Silent night, holy night!
Shepherds quake at the sight;
Glories stream from heaven afar,
Heav'nly hosts sing, Alleluia!
  Christ, the Savior, is born!
  Christ, the Savior, is born!

Silent night, holy night!
Son of God, love's pure light
Radiant beams from Thy holy face
With the dawn of redeeming grace,
  Jesus, Lord, at Thy birth,
  Jesus, Lord, at Thy birth.

Silent Night, Holy Night

Infant Holy, Infant Lowly

Infant holy,
  Infant lowly,
For His bed a cattle stall;
  Oxen lowing,
  Little knowing
Christ the child is Lord of all.
  Swiftly winging,
  Angels singing,
  Bells are ringing,
  Tidings bringing:
Christ the child is Lord of all!
Christ the child is Lord of all!

Flocks were sleeping,
  Shepherds keeping
Vigil till the morning new
  Saw the glory,
  Heard the story,
Tidings of a Gospel true.
  Thus rejoicing,
  Free from sorrow,
  Praises voicing,
  Greet the morrow:
Christ the child was born for you!
Christ the child was born for you!

Christ
the
Child is
LORD
of all!

And an angel of the Lord appeared to them, and the glory of the Lord shone around them, and they were filled with great fear. And the angel said to them, "Fear not, for behold, I bring you good news of great joy that will be for all the people. For unto you is born this day in the city of David a Savior, who is Christ the Lord."

(Luke 2:9–11)

In the cold, dark winter, evergreens are reminders of life. At Christmas, evergreens acknowledge eternal life as the gift of the Christ Child. The holly is especially meaningful as its features point not only to Christmas but also to Christ's Passion. Its red berries are symbols of Jesus' blood, shed on the cross for our sins. The points on the leaves are reminders of the crown of thorns placed on Jesus' head. In nature, the holly berry sustains birds during harsh winter months. This, too, reminds us of the sustenance we receive from the Lord: "You open Your hand; You satisfy the desire of every living thing" (Psalm 145:16).

Christ
the
Lord

Angels We Have Heard on High

Angels we have heard on high,
  Sweetly singing o'er the plains,
And the mountains in reply,
  Echoing their joyous strains. *REFRAIN*

REFRAIN:
Gloria in excelsis Deo.
Gloria in excelsis Deo.

Shepherds, why this jubilee?
  Why your joyous strains prolong?
What the gladsome tidings be
  Which inspire your heav'nly song? *REFRAIN*

Come to Bethlehem and see
  Him whose birth the angels sing;
Come, adore on bended knee
  Christ the Lord, the newborn King. *REFRAIN*

Gloria
in excelsis Deo!

Hark! The Herald Angels Sing

Hark! The herald angels sing,
"Glory to the newborn King;
Peace on earth and mercy mild,
God and sinners reconciled!"
Joyful, all ye nations, rise,
Join the triumph of the skies;
With the angelic host proclaim,
"Christ is born in Bethlehem!" *REFRAIN*

REFRAIN:
Hark! The herald angels sing,
"Glory to the newborn King!"

Christ, by highest heav'n adored,
Christ, the everlasting Lord,
Late in time behold Him come,
Offspring of a virgin's womb.
Veiled in flesh the Godhead see,
Hail the incarnate Deity!
Pleased as Man with man to dwell,
Jesus, our Immanuel! *REFRAIN*

Hail, the heav'n-born Prince of Peace!
Hail, the Sun of Righteousness!
Light and life to all He brings,
Ris'n with healing in His wings.
Mild He lays His glory by,
Born that man no more may die,
Born to raise the sons of earth,
Born to give them second birth. *REFRAIN*

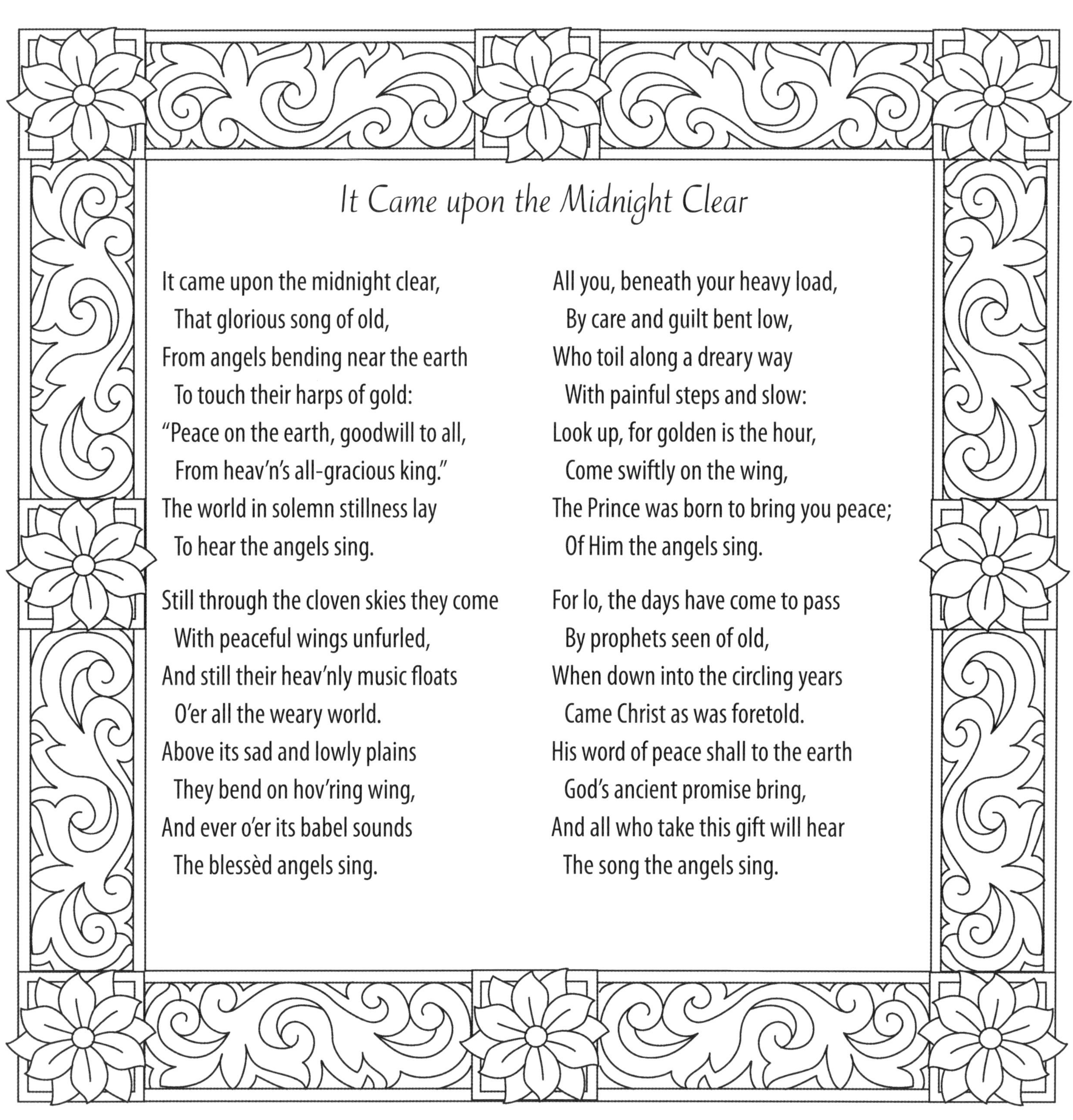

It Came upon the Midnight Clear

It came upon the midnight clear,
  That glorious song of old,
From angels bending near the earth
  To touch their harps of gold:
"Peace on the earth, goodwill to all,
  From heav'n's all-gracious king."
The world in solemn stillness lay
  To hear the angels sing.

Still through the cloven skies they come
  With peaceful wings unfurled,
And still their heav'nly music floats
  O'er all the weary world.
Above its sad and lowly plains
  They bend on hov'ring wing,
And ever o'er its babel sounds
  The blessèd angels sing.

All you, beneath your heavy load,
  By care and guilt bent low,
Who toil along a dreary way
  With painful steps and slow:
Look up, for golden is the hour,
  Come swiftly on the wing,
The Prince was born to bring you peace;
  Of Him the angels sing.

For lo, the days have come to pass
  By prophets seen of old,
When down into the circling years
  Came Christ as was foretold.
His word of peace shall to the earth
  God's ancient promise bring,
And all who take this gift will hear
  The song the angels sing.

And suddenly there was with the angel a multitude
of the heavenly host praising God and saying,
"Glory to God in the highest,
and on earth peace among those with
whom He is pleased!"

(Luke 2:13–14)

GLORY
to
GOD

Angels from the Realms of Glory

Angels from the realms of glory,
  Wing your flight o'er all the earth;
Ye who sang creation's story,
  Now proclaim Messiah's birth. *REFRAIN*

REFRAIN:
Come and worship, come and worship;
Worship Christ, the newborn King.

Shepherds in the field abiding,
  Watching o'er your flocks by night,
God with us is now residing,
  Yonder shines the Infant Light. *REFRAIN*

Sages, leave your contemplations,
  Brighter visions beam afar;
Seek the great Desire of nations,
  Ye have seen His natal star. *REFRAIN*

Saints before the altar bending,
  Watching long in hope and fear,
Suddenly the Lord, descending,
  In His temple shall appear. *REFRAIN*

All creation, join in praising
  God the Father, Spirit, Son,
Evermore your voices raising
  To the eternal Three in One. *REFRAIN*

In a manger Jesus lies;
Angels praise Him in the skies.
Shepherds kneel before Him low.
To His stable let us go.
Light of heaven and Morning Star,
Dear Lord Jesus, Thine we are.
Lead us as Thy very own
To the Father's shining throne.

Joy to the World

Joy to the world, the Lord is come!
Let earth receive her King;
Let ev'ry heart prepare Him room
And heav'n and nature sing,
And heav'n and nature sing,
And heav'n, and heav'n and nature sing.

Joy to the earth, the Savior reigns!
Let men their songs employ,
While fields and floods, rocks, hills, and plains
Repeat the sounding joy,
Repeat the sounding joy,
Repeat, repeat the sounding joy.

No more let sins and sorrows grow
Nor thorns infest the ground;
He comes to make His blessings flow
Far as the curse is found,
Far as the curse is found,
Far as, far as the curse is found.

He rules the world with truth and grace
And makes the nations prove
The glories of His righteousness
And wonders of His love,
And wonders of His love,
And wonders, wonders of His love.

JOY
to the World

When the angels went away from them into heaven, the shepherds said to one another, "Let us go over to Bethlehem and see this thing that has happened, which the Lord has made known to us."

(Luke 2:15)

Once in Royal David's City

Once in royal David's city
  Stood a lowly cattle shed,
Where a mother laid her baby
  In a manger for His bed:
Mary was that mother mild,
Jesus Christ her little child.

He came down to earth from heaven,
  Who is God and Lord of all,
And His shelter was a stable,
  And His cradle was a stall;
With the poor and mean and lowly
Lived on earth our Savior holy.

For He is our childhood's pattern,
  Day by day like us He grew;
He was little, weak, and helpless,
  Tears and smiles like us He knew;
And He feels for all our sadness,
And He shares in all our gladness.

And our eyes at last shall see Him,
  Through His own redeeming love;
For that child so dear and gentle
  Is our Lord in heav'n above;
And He leads His children on
To the place where He is gone.

Not in that poor, lowly stable
  With the oxen standing by
Shall we see Him, but in heaven,
  Set at God's right hand on high.
Then like stars His children, crowned,
All in white, His praise will sound!

And they went with haste and found Mary and Joseph,
and the baby lying in the manger.
(Luke 2:16)

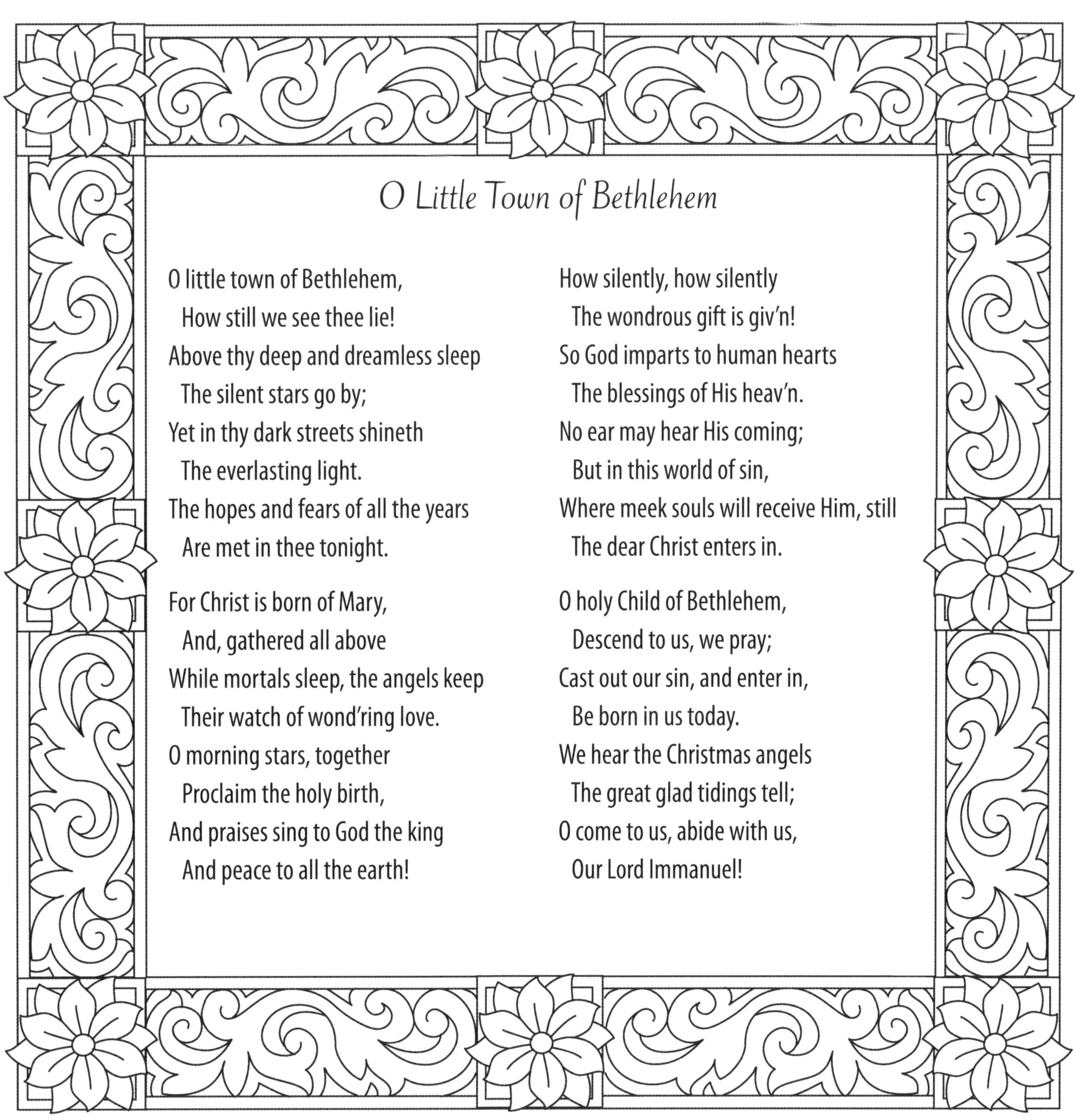

O Little Town of Bethlehem

O little town of Bethlehem,
How still we see thee lie!
Above thy deep and dreamless sleep
The silent stars go by;
Yet in thy dark streets shineth
The everlasting light.
The hopes and fears of all the years
Are met in thee tonight.

For Christ is born of Mary,
And, gathered all above
While mortals sleep, the angels keep
Their watch of wond'ring love.
O morning stars, together
Proclaim the holy birth,
And praises sing to God the king
And peace to all the earth!

How silently, how silently
The wondrous gift is giv'n!
So God imparts to human hearts
The blessings of His heav'n.
No ear may hear His coming;
But in this world of sin,
Where meek souls will receive Him, still
The dear Christ enters in.

O holy Child of Bethlehem,
Descend to us, we pray;
Cast out our sin, and enter in,
Be born in us today.
We hear the Christmas angels
The great glad tidings tell;
O come to us, abide with us,
Our Lord Immanuel!

Now Sing We, Now Rejoice

Now sing we, now rejoice,
Now raise to heav'n our voice;
He from whom joy streameth
Poor in a manger lies;
Not so brightly beameth
The sun in yonder skies.
Thou my Savior art!
Thou my Savior art!

Come from on high to me;
I cannot rise to Thee.
Cheer my wearied spirit,
O pure and holy Child;
Through Thy grace and merit,
Blest Jesus, Lord most mild,
Draw me unto Thee!
Draw me unto Thee!

Now through His Son doth shine
The Father's grace divine.
Death was reigning o'er us
Through sin and vanity
Till He opened for us
A bright eternity.
May we praise Him there!
May we praise Him there!

Oh, where shall joy be found?
Where but on heav'nly ground?
Where the angels singing
With all His saints unite,
Sweetest praises bringing
In heav'nly joy and light.
Oh, that we were there!
Oh, that we were there!

In the beginning, God created the sun as the greater light. In the natural world, sunlight brings growth and is crucial to life. In eternity, the Light of the world, Jesus, takes us to "a bright eternity." Scripture is rich with sun imagery in relation to the Son of God. For example, we read in 2 Corinthians 4:6, "For God, who said, 'Let light shine out of darkness,' has shone in our hearts to give the light of the knowledge of the glory of God in the face of Jesus Christ." Because of this, we rejoice.

And behold, the star that they had seen when it rose went before them until it came to rest over the place where the child was.

(Matthew 2:9)

What Child Is This

What child is this, who, laid to rest,
  On Mary's lap is sleeping?
Whom angels greet with anthems sweet
  While shepherds watch are keeping?
This, this is Christ the king,
Whom shepherds guard and angels sing;
  Haste, haste to bring Him laud,
  The babe, the son of Mary!

Why lies He in such mean estate
  Where ox and ass are feeding?
Good Christian, fear; for sinners here
  The silent Word is pleading.
Nails, spear shall pierce Him through,
The cross be borne for me, for you;
  Hail, hail the Word made flesh,
  The babe, the son of Mary!

So bring Him incense, gold, and myrrh;
  Come, peasant, king, to own Him.
The King of kings salvation brings;
  Let loving hearts enthrone Him.
Raise, raise the song on high,
The virgin sings her lullaby;
  Joy, joy, for Christ is born,
  The babe, the son of Mary!

King
of kings

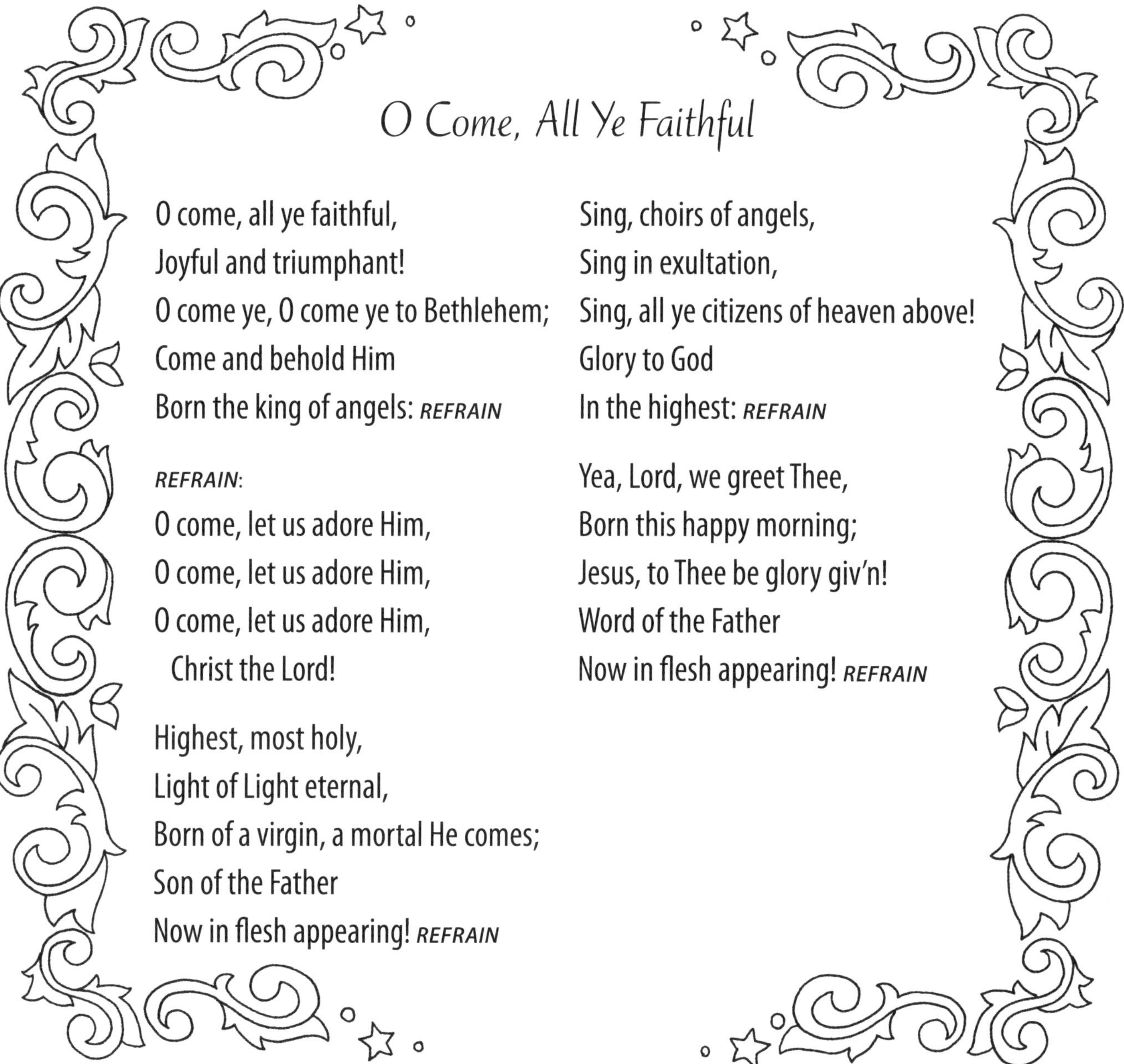

O Come, All Ye Faithful

O come, all ye faithful,
Joyful and triumphant!
O come ye, O come ye to Bethlehem;
Come and behold Him
Born the king of angels: *REFRAIN*

REFRAIN:
O come, let us adore Him,
O come, let us adore Him,
O come, let us adore Him,
Christ the Lord!

Highest, most holy,
Light of Light eternal,
Born of a virgin, a mortal He comes;
Son of the Father
Now in flesh appearing! *REFRAIN*

Sing, choirs of angels,
Sing in exultation,
Sing, all ye citizens of heaven above!
Glory to God
In the highest: *REFRAIN*

Yea, Lord, we greet Thee,
Born this happy morning;
Jesus, to Thee be glory giv'n!
Word of the Father
Now in flesh appearing! *REFRAIN*

A legend from Mexico is responsible for our use of the poinsettia at Christmas. According to this legend, a young girl on her way to a Christmas Eve worship service picked a handful of a common weed to lay at the altar as a gift for the baby Jesus. When an angel saw the child's sincere gift, he changed the green weed to a red flower. The shape of the flower is said to resemble the star of Bethlehem, the red leaves are said to symbolize the blood of Christ, and the white flowers remind us of Christ's sinlessness.

JOY
Glory
Joy
Glory
JOY
GLORY
JOY

And when they saw the star, they rejoiced exceedingly with great joy. And going into the house they saw the child with Mary His mother, and they fell down and worshiped Him. Then, opening their treasures, they offered Him gifts, gold and frankincense and myrrh.
(Matthew 2:10–11)

Of the Father's Love Begotten

Of the Father's love begotten
  Ere the worlds began to be,
He is Alpha and Omega,
  He the source, the ending He,
Of the things that are, that have been,
  And that future years shall see
  Evermore and evermore.

Oh, that birth forever blessèd,
  When the virgin, full of grace,
By the Holy Ghost conceiving,
  Bore the Savior of our race,
And the babe, the world's Redeemer,
  First revealed His sacred face
  Evermore and evermore.

This is He whom seers in old time
  Chanted of with one accord,
Whom the voices of the prophets
  Promised in their faithful word.
Now He shines, the long-expected;
  Let creation praise its Lord
  Evermore and evermore.

O ye heights of heav'n, adore Him;
  Angel hosts, His praises sing.
Pow'rs, dominions, bow before Him
  And extol our God and King.
Let no tongue on earth be silent,
  Ev'ry voice in concert ring
  Evermore and evermore.

Christ, to Thee, with God the Father,
  And, O Holy Ghost, to Thee
Hymn and chant and high thanksgiving
  And unending praises be,
Honor, glory, and dominion,
  And eternal victory
  Evermore and evermore.

Amen.

Written by Prudentius, a fourth-century poet, this hymn is considered by some to be the first great hymn to make the case for the Trinity. The first line in Latin—*Corde natus ex parentis ante mundi exordium*—means, literally, "born from the parent's heart before the beginning of time." The last line of each stanza emphasizes the eternal nature of God. The illustration, therefore, incorporates the symbols of the Alpha and the Omega, the first and last letters of the Greek alphabet. This represents completeness and fullness. Jesus calls Himself the Alpha and the Omega (Revelation 1:8). From this we understand that Jesus is the eternal Word of God. Also notice the triquetra in the illustration, the ancient symbol for the Trinity that communicates the eternal nature of God.

As with Gladness Men of Old

As with gladness men of old
Did the guiding star behold;
  As with joy they hailed its light,
  Leading onward, beaming bright;
So, most gracious Lord, may we
Evermore be led by Thee.

As with joyful steps they sped,
Savior, to Thy lowly bed,
  There to bend the knee before
  Thee, whom heav'n and earth adore;
So may we with willing feet
Ever seek Thy mercy seat.

As they offered gifts most rare
At Thy cradle, rude and bare,
  So may we with holy joy,
  Pure and free from sin's alloy,
All our costliest treasures bring,
Christ, to Thee, our heav'nly King.

Holy Jesus, ev'ry day
Keep us in the narrow way;
  And when earthly things are past,
  Bring our ransomed souls at last
Where they need no star to guide,
Where no clouds Thy glory hide.

In the heav'nly country bright
Need they no created light;
  Thou its light, its joy, its crown,
  Thou its sun which goes not down;
There forever may we sing
Alleluias to our King.

Christmas isn't only
A decorated tree,
Holly wreaths and evergreen,
And gifts for you and me.

Christmas is remembering
A night so long ago,
A little town called Bethlehem,
A manger bed so low.

Christmas is remembering
The Baby on the hay.
That little one is God's own Son,
Our Savior, born that day.

Christmas is remembering
Why He came down to earth,
Why God gave us His only Son,
The reason for Christ's birth.

Christmas is remembering
The cross on which He died
For You, for me, for all of us,
Christ Jesus Crucified!

But when the fullness of time had come, God sent forth His Son, born of woman, born under the law, to redeem those who were under the law, so that we might receive adoption as sons.

(Galatians 4:4–5)

Nicholas was a pastor in fourth-century Lycia, what is modern-day Turkey. As word of his generosity spread to Europe, he became known as Father Christmas (and in America, Santa Claus). Legends about his home at the North Pole and distributing gifts on Christmas Eve were created to enhance his story, but his generosity is based in historical fact.

Many families observe St. Nicholas Day on the sixth of December when the children of the household awaken to find gold foil-wrapped chocolate coins in their shoes.

The kindness and care Saint Nicholas showed are examples we can learn from. He gave gifts out of thankfulness for the greatest gift of all, our Savior Jesus Christ.

Songs of Thankfulness and Praise

Songs of thankfulness and praise,
Jesus, Lord, to Thee we raise,
  Manifested by the star
  To the sages from afar,
Branch of royal David's stem
In Thy birth at Bethlehem:
  Anthems be to Thee addressed,
  God in man made manifest.

Manifest at Jordan's stream,
Prophet, Priest, and King supreme;
  And at Cana wedding guest
  In Thy Godhead manifest;
Manifest in pow'r divine,
Changing water into wine;
  Anthems be to Thee addressed,
  God in man made manifest.

Manifest in making whole
Palsied limbs and fainting soul;
  Manifest in valiant fight,
  Quelling all the devil's might;
Manifest in gracious will,
Ever bringing good from ill;
  Anthems be to Thee addressed,
  God in man made manifest.

Sun and moon shall darkened be,
Stars shall fall, the heav'ns shall flee;
  Christ will then like lightning shine,
  All will see His glorious sign;
All will then the trumpet hear,
All will see the Judge appear;
  Thou by all wilt be confessed,
  God in man made manifest.

Grant us grace to see Thee, Lord,
Present in Thy holy Word—
  Grace to imitate Thee now
  And be pure, as pure art Thou;
That we might become like Thee
At Thy great epiphany
  And may praise Thee, ever blest,
  God in man made manifest.

The word *manifest* is key to understanding the message and imagery of this hymn. The simple definition is "to clearly show or demonstrate." Here we acknowledge our praise and thanksgiving for the fulfillment of God's promise of a Savior manifested in Christ's birth, His Baptism, His works on earth, and His victory over the devil. Illustrated here are manifestations of God's love for us in Jesus—His Word, the Bible, and the Lord's Supper—graciously given to us in abundance.

Arise, shine, for your light has come,
And the glory of the Lord has risen upon you.

(Isaiah 60:1)

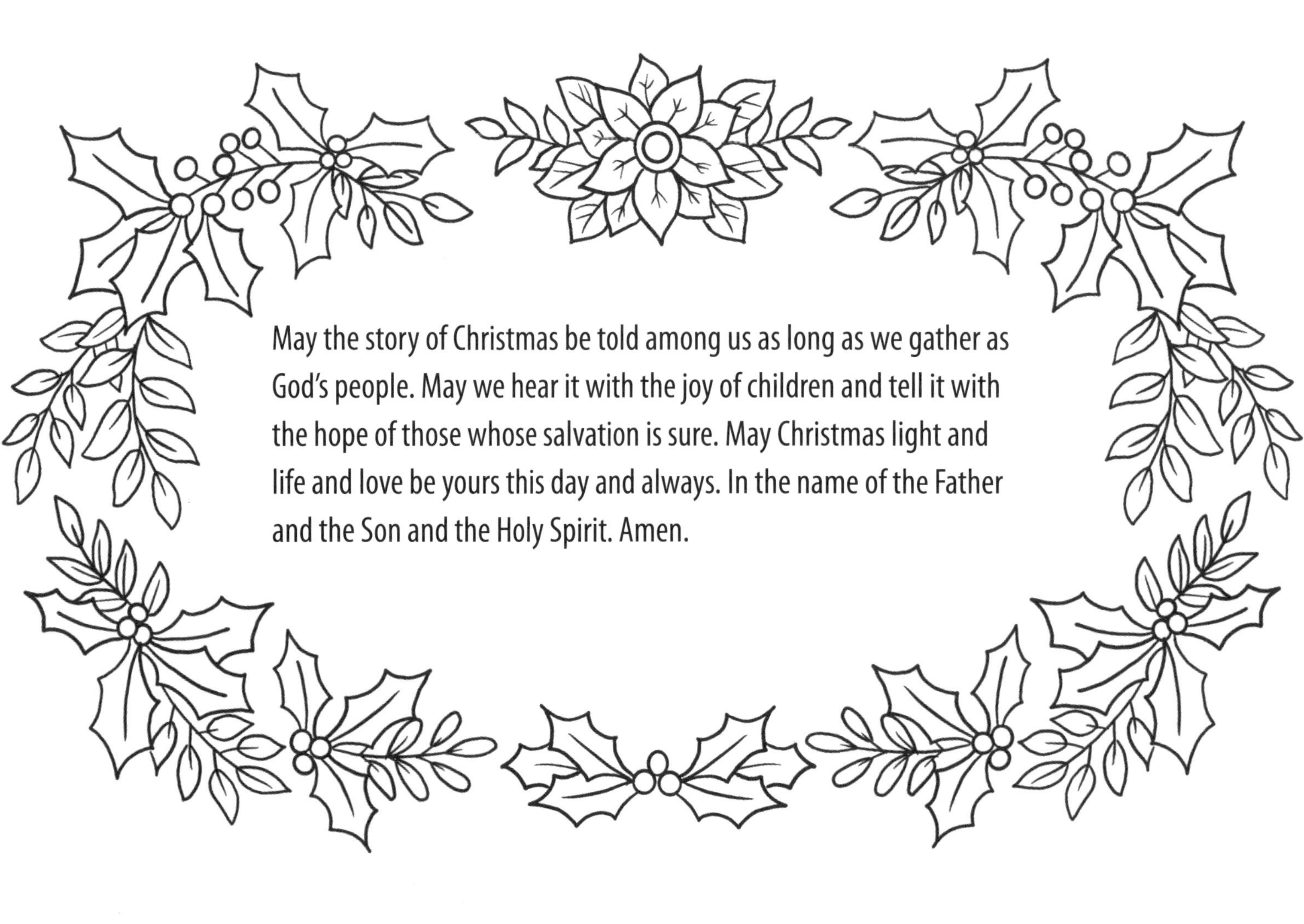

May the story of Christmas be told among us as long as we gather as God's people. May we hear it with the joy of children and tell it with the hope of those whose salvation is sure. May Christmas light and life and love be yours this day and always. In the name of the Father and the Son and the Holy Spirit. Amen.